POETRY
now

Across The Skies

Edited by

Heather Killingray

First published in Great Britain in 2003 by
POETRY NOW
Remus House,
Coltsfoot Drive,
Peterborough, PE2 9JX
Telephone (01733) 898101
Fax (01733) 313524

HB ISBN 0 75434 429 0
SB ISBN 0 75434 430 4

FOREWORD

Although we are a nation of poets we are accused of not reading poetry, or buying poetry books. After many years of listening to the incessant gripes of poetry publishers, I can only assume that the books they publish, in general, are books that most people do not want to read.

Poetry should not be obscure, introverted, and as cryptic as a crossword puzzle: it is the poet's duty to reach out and embrace the world.

The world owes the poet nothing and we should not be expected to dig and delve into a rambling discourse searching for some inner meaning.

The reason we write poetry (and almost all of us do) is because we want to communicate: an ideal; an idea; or a specific feeling. Poetry is as essential in communication, as a letter; a radio; a telephone, and the main criterion for selecting the poems in this anthology is very simple: they communicate.

CONTENTS

NEXT TIME ROUND . . .

(Dedicated to my mom, my sister and myself!)

As soon as I've put the washing away
There's another load waiting for me
Just when I've dried the last dinner plate
It's almost time for tea!

When the house has been polished from bottom to top
The dust has settled again
As soon as the windows are cleaned and buffed
It always starts to rain!

No sooner I've put the vacuum away
Crumbs appear on the floor
Just when I've finished mowing the grass
The weeds have grown once more!

As soon as I put my toe in the bath
There's someone at the door
The telephone only stops ringing
When I'm dripping all over the floor!

As soon as my head hits the pillow
The alarm clock starts to ring
The dark's already turned to light
And birds have started to sing!

I'm a multi-talented woman
I can do ten things at once
Jack of all trades and master of none
So now, here comes the crunch!

I'll meet myself coming back one day
And start where I began
But if given a choice, then next time round
I'm coming back as a man!

Jo-Ann Waldron-Hall

BUTTERFLIES

I never knew him -
Or where he went,
But I'll never forget his face,
His smile - or the look in his eyes.

He was on the train -
An old steam train it was.
He was leaning from the window
As people used to on steam trains.
I was on the platform
Having just arrived -
He was going on somewhere.
Somehow I caught his glance
And just for a fleeting moment
My heart leapt -
And butterflies danced -

He felt it too -
I saw surprise in his eyes
A startled expression -
He raised his hand,
Then he and the train were gone.

That was many years ago -
I've never forgotten,
It makes me smile,
I sometimes wonder if he thinks of me
As I have thought of him?

Leonie Lewis Park

THANK YOU

Thank you, for being you,
This is what I have to say,
There's never been no one like you,
You surely make my day.

You're sweet and kind and gentle,
In everything you do,
But most of all; you're wonderful,
So thank you for being you.

E B Holcombe

SENIOR MISTRESS

I can see her now . . .
Advancing down the school corridor
Academic gown billowing
Students and staff quailing at the sight
Senior Mistress in full flight.

In her wake, the work-shy, the troublemakers
Clutching punishment lines
Departing her orbit hastily, thankfully,
Lessons learned.

Bird-like, her physique misleads
Hints at weakness, frailty.
Forget it!
This is a zero-tolerance lady.

From the raised stronghold of the teacher's dais
Her four feet eleven inches
Meets six footers eyeball to eyeball.
Steely-blue eyes alert for dissemblance
Spots a shirker at twenty paces.

French teacher par excellence
Eccentric perhaps,
Dedicated without doubt
Educational equality her aim
When will we see her like again?

Vera Morrill

TIME

Time is on my side
Time is on yours
My heart waves with the tide
The tears, the ache my heart pours
Time is precious, love is too
Passes so quick, heartache through
And through
Oh! I wish this pain would pass
Wake me up from this dream
Woe, sadness, alas!
To wish things were different
So supreme
No hurt, no pain
To re-live, to repeat again
Change the choices
Get rid of the voices
(Haunting voices)
Change the past
Peace at last.

C Degan

Weather Blues

My stomach feels like fluffy snow
My heart feels like hailstones
My legs are stuck in the mud
My head is in a storm
How can I feel like this, just one day on?

Yesterday you came into my life
Flashing lightning all around
The excitement of thunder felt deep down
Drizzle running down my spine
How can I feel like this? We have just met.

Should I tell you how I feel
Will the heavy rain wash these feelings away
Should I wait, will I see you again
Will you shower me with love
Should I leave it to fate
How can I feel like this? Are you my soulmate?

Denise Bannister

The Clouds

A cloud of cloth floating,
Soaring and singing
Upon the breeze.
Woven from the creamy fleece,
From blessed angels' wings,
Mid dreams, where suns
And spirits flee.
As sweet sunset starts to breathe,
Surrendering her eve, unseen
Over mountains and streams.

While the sunken sun, sighs
And falls, from the sky,
Like a fading sphere,
In silence and shame,
Its melody now faint.
Shadow breezes, cold and grey,
Are lifted and spirited away.
Lapped inside a tender light
That grows bright,
From this weary world, of strife.

Shirley Kelleher

THIS SCOTLAND

This sacred land of lochs and braes,
Mountains high and castles old.
Where mighty battles raged and fought,
By knights and armies brave and bold.
Pretty coloured heather covering the ground,
Rugged landscapes stretching on for miles and miles.
Can you hear the bagpipes?
Their mournful sound,
across the highlands cold and wild.
The deer so timid come down to graze below,
When the mountain top's thick with winter's snow.
Icy rivers rush to meet the foaming seas,
Scotland, a land of past great kings and queens.
Many bonnie lasses dance,
a swirl of tartan,
the spirit of this land.
So raise a glass you noble clansmen,
A wee dram for them all - Scotland the brave!
Then I will surely hurry back
to this land where salmon leap,
and eagles soar.

Dorothy Chadwick

THANK YOU

As I lie in bed
Can't help but stare
Into that big empty
Space
Joyful moments
Shared with you
Couldn't wait to get
Home at night
You sleeping peacefully
All curled up
I love to watch you dream
Wondering if blissful play
Was your creation
Always got your way
The king of your
Own kingdom
Gonna miss your
Glossy black eyes
That showed so much
Happiness
Your white and black
Soft to touch fur
That pink ropey tail
That you often stood on
In excitement
When you get to Heaven
Don't forget me, because
I certainly
Won't forget you.

Rachel Baldwin

Tess

Tess, she may have felt
momentarily relieved,
when Angel Clare confessed, to her, his sins.
Her own offence,
logic led her to deduce,
could not be any worse, for
''tis the same'.
Oh Tess, you foolish girl. Unfeigned
naiveté *always* was uncool.
The pattern remains the same; always
will do.
I forgive you; now I ask the same of you.
While we were apart,
I was human, too.
But, darling, don't you know? How could you
not see? 'Human' is synonymous with 'man',
in this context.
Angel C's 'sins' were
conquests. Call it sexual
discrimination, if you will.
Women always get the worst deal.

Paula Puddephatt

JUST PEACE

If I could have my wish
My wish
Would surely be
For peace
All over the planet
A world war-torn free
I'd wish for all the peoples
To come together as one
No wars, no anger, no hatred
Just peace for everyone.

Greeny 2002

RIBBON OF LIGHT

Shimmering in the golden sunlight
On its journey to the sea,
River, full of mixed emotions,
Creates a peace within me.
Reflections dancing on the ripples,
Stirred by gentle summer breeze.
Minnows play amongst the rushes,
Distant drone of honeybees.
Over weed-strewn rocks it tumbles,
Gurgling gaily on its way.
Dragonflies skimming the surface
On rainbowed wings their skills display.
In mellow mood it meanders idly,
Winding through the hills and vales,
But when aroused it rents its fury,
Tormented by rainstorms and gales.
Translucent ribbon bound for freedom,
Kindles passions of the heart.
Hopes and dreams float there before you,
Time erased, a world apart.

Sue Mackenzie

10 MONTHS HARD LABOUR

Here I lie immersed in comatose,
Oppressed, I dream of escape.
Basking in static confusion,
Who strikes hard on obsessive lies.
I embark on self-discovery,
Inflicting realities of previously untold truths.
No sterner judge than oneself,
Who else can see all deeds obscured from strangers' eyes?
The outside world is a distant memory,
I am imprisoned here within my own thoughts.
Questioning every past action,
Fighting absolution from my harshest critic.
Please wake me,
I cannot face myself.
The only person I can't deceive,
The person who knows me best.
Unrelenting,
I will be punished.

Jondaniel Harris

Fate

A tiny baby, always there, he's never changed
Many years now, he's always there
I thought I knew, I thought you had told me
But no, he's still there
Who is he? He cries, you're there, how can it be?

Years later I see him, but this scene is too familiar
This one wakes me screaming, my baby boy he's screaming
He looks right at us, his eyes are dead, he hears the planes
But how? How is it possible? He's not even imagined yet
How can he be there? That was years ago

Why do I see it, is it real?
I am crazy, oh God noooooo
One day I know I will hold him, my arms ache for him
My brain says it's horrors and dreams
My heart says it's love and truth
My mind says it's a gift, he's returning to you

I'm scared, I want to know, I don't like the unknown
This child, so many years he's been here, in my heart
Each pregnancy I've awaited his arrival
Each time I've given a male child his name
But yet, no male has appeared

What is he? Why do I see him?
Why do I feel him?
I know you feel him
How long must I wait for my son
Will he ever come
Or is he just in my mind?
Nothing more than an electrical impulse
Or is he more, so much more, is he . . .

Fate.

Agnes Neeson

DEEP INSIDE ME IS A CANDLE

Deep inside me is a candle
Burning clear as starry night
But while it stays alone inside me
It is such a little light

I wait for one to touch me
Who can light the love in here
Make it burn like supernova
Make it burn like sunlight clear

Take this little light of loving
Make it shine out of the grey
Like a million shining fireflies
At the closing of the day

Turn the glimmer in the shadows
To a starburst in the sky
With a little of your loving
As a comet flying by

As the candle deep inside me
Becomes a searing flame so bright
It is fuelled by the true love
That turned darkness into light

Paul Knox

One Surrounding World

To feel love would be the greatest feeling to have
never knowing where your heart will take you next
feeling like you could fly in the sky every waking day of your life

To smell a flower that your true love has sent
and keeping that smell with you at all times
because that's the smell you've been longing for

To hear his voice, to touch and kiss his lips
these are the things you want with you forever
these are the true things that never leave your side

To taste the hunger of life whenever you're with him
and before never knowing you could have this one life
yet knowing in your heart you once would

To see his eyes light up whenever he's around you
gives you a floating feeling in your body and soul
while slowly falling into a state of honour and love

Let your senses guide you to the one you're meant for
this means let every sense lead the way
and this is what I believe will happen to me someday

Katie Jewitt (18)

TREE

One beech tree bows its head, bows to the east.
Knows it bows to the east?
A hundred years of growing have surely earned it wisdom,
a deep arboreal knowing of the ways of the wind.

A hundred years. A million leaves have burst their buds and lived,
each for one season, feeling the wind's sigh, its gusty cough,
those cruel, equinoctial gales.

Felt too the warmth of the wandering sun;
felt the dew, the rain, the snow and hail.
Does not each move and moment register in those leaves
as in the nerve ends of a sentient life?

A world of life: gnats' home, bees' home;
home to a thousand grubs and bugs and creepy-crawly things;
perch of the braggart thrush
that sweetens the evening spring.

Here on your boughs the monstrous owl
waits for its meal of mouse.
Life gnaws your roots; rots in the annual litter of leaves.
Tonight a full, fat moon will fill again the eastern sky
behind the trinity of cairns which guard a Neolithic hill.

Can these many, many lives have sown no knowledge
in your flowing, flowering universe?

Here in your shade we intertwine, my love and I
and see with lovers' eyes
and feel with lovers' nerves
and smile because we know, old tree:
we know you know.

Richard Frost

BULLY

You approach me one day
With a gang by your side,
I'm feeling so scared,
I just want to hide.
You're shouting words
To make me feel bad,
I won't go outside,
I'm feeling so sad.
All through my life,
right into school,
I put up with bullies
Who were evil and cruel.
They made me feel worthless,
I knew they were wrong,
All of my hurt,
I could write in a song.
So what is a bully?
This cannot be right
And how can you possibly
Sleep at night?
I could not care less
About someone like you,
Becoming a bully
Will never be new.
I look at your life
And laugh in your face,
I'll never forget
Your jealousy, hate.
So be a bad person,
See if I care,
I'm moving on up.
So where are you?
Where?

R Gallagher

FREEDOM

The bundle lay by the side of the road,
The cars passed by, one by one,
Even the birds in the sky moved on,
No one stopped,
No one cared,
With his last breath he spoke one word,
Freedom,
With that the trees began to cover him
With a quilt of leaves,
As his spirit passed from one world
To the next,
Freedom.

Andy Powell

A Lover's Dream

I see your face.
I look in your eyes.
I think about all the selfish lies
That you told me,
To get to know me?
That's your excuse,
Then why don't you show me.
The girls, the girls that you know,
Or the ones that you would go out with,
Just for the night,
A one night stand,
You'd better treat me right.

Cos, I've seen the damage
That you've done.
I bet you've been with everyone in town
And don't you frown at me,
As though you don't know what I mean.
You know that I love you
And I hope that you love me too.
Do you care, when you stare
If I'm in trouble,
Will you be there?

I look in your eyes and move closer
As I kiss you on the lips.
We sway from side to side
With your arms around my hips.
We move around the room
Like lovers dancing in the rain.
I want to kiss your smile
And feel all the joy and pain.

I need to know that you love me
And I want to know the truth.
I don't need any evidence,
I don't need any proof.

I will take your word for it,
Cos I enjoy every bit.
Or is it more than it may seem?
A lover's dream.

Helen Davis

EXTINCTION

Our footprints in the snow
Mark our passing;
Fine flakes flurrying
Soon descend and hastily hide our tracks;
Our presence is forever obliterated.

Liam Heaney

White Palms
(Part 1)

Waves lash the concrete plinths -
Obscenities cast in foreign stone -
Foundations of the new world.
Whose new world?
What was wrong with the old one?
The white sands and the rock pools.
The mangroves and the swamps?
Where will the oysters grow?
What will happen
To the women who gather them -
The men who burn and grind the shells -
The children who mix the white powder
With the salt water
To make emulsion:
To paint the bricks -
White man's bricks
To build the white house
And white hotel
With hands that are black -
But not with dirt?

Susan Seward

Sweat City

Sweat City - simmering - summer heat -
Deciding - window open - gaping - down on the city -
Air pervading - TVs, radios blaring -
Tunes playing - songs taking - evening -
Drinking - refreshing - all
Singing - all dancing - forehead
Glistening - inside - heat - night calling -
Perfect timing - evening - through - warm imperceptibly cooling.

C J Bayless

The Untouched Day

I sit dreaming of the untouched day
When everything is pure and good
Without the killing of this word
I can be happy, free from troubles
Somewhere to laugh and dance
If I lived in the untouched day.

With the wind blowing through my hair
The sun up high in the sky
Birds singing their tunes, a skylark, hark
Cats dancing on clouds, what fun
Floating over hill and vale, a rainbow for my bed
A will-of-the-wisp no one could see.

If I lived in the untouched day
I would be me with no substance
Dancing with the elves and fairies
No one would see me, I would be *me*
I could make it mine, a sanctuary
If I lived in the untouched day.

A bumblebee would be my friend
I would stroke his strips of yellow
That day would be just perfect
I could dance with a beautiful fox
If I lived in the untouched day
A place I could go to, suspended in time.

My retreat, 'The Untouched Day.'

Carole A Cleverdon

NEVER GROW UP - ONLY OUTWARD!

The fairies have been
In my garden.
They had a party
Last night.
They know that summer
Is over,
From the colours that
Do surround.
They've scattered them under
The treetops
To make such a pretty sight
And magic'ly dusted
The mushrooms
With fairy dew
So bright.
The grasses are waving
So gladly.
The berries now
Have a shine.
And so those fairies
Are happy
Because their garden
Is mine!

Lyn Sandford

Ghost

Don't disappear,
because even in the dark, with my eyes tight shut and blindfold,
colours ballet through my sight,
fleetingly oblivious to the absence of the light.

And somewhere an old friend plays his guitar
and sings. It's been years
but I can still hear gravity hollowing him out
and sounding him off; still see
that ragged chin and upper lip
mouth the opinion that *Brolly* would be a great name for a dog.
Or *Gish.*

Don't disappear, because it's years before
your weightless ghost might wake me, in tears,
from some blank state of sleep,
yet I can't see you anymore.

So that's all I'll have,
love,
of you.

Just that.

Samuel Kindred

SPLITS

I'm trapped in my bodily existence
By a zombie am I occupied
A spectre I cannot see
Inside of me
That no one notices
Nor can I notice truly

At night this zombie leaves the self
And roams somewhere
O'er dale and lea
My consciousness it thwarts to a degree
A spook no one believes in
No one? No one but me

I lived long in the shade of self
Unnoticed then
Not demanding notice I ran
I think therefore I am - or can
But does my zombie think?
He walks alone, the shadow of a man

Into the dark he goes
A phantom with no heart
Still the heart of something beats
In the impalpable seats
Of another life
Deserting self, life my zombie greets.

Angus Richmond

It Is Not You

How can I love
You
When all I see is
Hate?

You say,
I'm
Passion;
Bearer of your heart.
Yet you push
Me away.

This is not the
Love
I'd dreamed of.
Catch my gaze;
Know it is not for
You.

Helen Walker

The Fool's Costume

(Sometimes laughter is the 'best medicine')

I am winter,
Cold and dead
With a cord
Around my head.

For Christmas,
I wear holly
On my stick
To be holy.

Nicola Barnes

Forces

There was darkness in the world
When chaos ruled
There was darkness in the world
When death ruled

The word was grim
When chaos ruled
The world was black
When death ruled

Hand in hand these forces created darkness
When chaos and death ruled
Evil beasts walked the Earth
When chaos and death ruled

But then from the darkness
Came joy
But then from the darkness
Came hope

Hand in hand these forces created light
When joy and hope ruled
Light returned to the Earth
When joy and hope ruled

Chaos was destroyed
When joy and hope ruled
Death was destroyed
When hope ruled.

There was light in the world
When joy ruled
There was light in the world
When hope ruled.

Matthew Routledge (13)

THE DISTANT FUTURE

A distant future, so far away my dreams still overtake my reality.
If I could travel to the future I would have all I need and want
for eternity.
But alas, I am stuck in this zone to wait for the life that awaits me to
catch up with my time, for if my future was my present I would have no
future, no life to look forward too.
Accept what you have and never let it go for things can change in an
instant and leave you full of happiness or leave you out in the cold.

Sara Clendinning

The Party

Oh Mother, I'll feel so shown up,
If I take Jam sandwiches for tea,
I know it's a birthday party,
But everyone will be talking about me.
I've not had any new clothes for ages,
Or a pair of new shoes to wear,
Isn't life really rotten, why does it have to be so unfair?
I've decided not to go to the party,
We'll have these sandwiches for tea
And tomorrow I'll have a look in Oxfam,
There might be some clothes to fit me.

James Ayrey

Vie Tulloch

Eighty-plus,
With attitude and aura half her age,
Vie is a lady who puts
An 'E' in vi(e)brant!
When young and smooth of skin,
She took gnarled wood,
Carved her stamp on it
As finest sculpture; shaping it
To echo her beliefs and faith.
They pose all o'er the land;
Their silken polish, soft, reflecting sheen
With powerful messages will be
Perpetual memorials to her,
While she now bears
The gnarls of venerable age.
Lone, but not lonely in her
Island cottage, looking seaward.
She's swift of mind, with gleaming eye
And dancing heart; and keeps
That joy and magic
Which draw folk to her
To sit with her
And be inspired!

Susan Grant

The Forgotten Butterfly

There was a bottle in the cellar
Corked so nothing could escape.
It lay among the dust and dirt,
A thing you'd think incapable of hurt.
It caught my eye one afternoon
And pushed me back through space and time.
I saw two children, one had found
A tiny chrysalis on the ground.
A flash of lightning came to me,
A memory. Too late! Too late!
Ten years too late. And yet
I struggled through the net of webs
And brushed the dirt and dust away
In search of yesterday.

Poor butterfly, so well preserved.
You came out full of hope
Into a barren world.
You never felt warm sunlight
Or landed on a flower.
You spent your life in darkness,
Trapped by my human power.

I corked you in. I didn't mean
To hurt you in your sleep.
I did it for the children
So they could watch you creep
Out of your chrysalis, transformed.
Instead, we all forgot you,
Trapped in your shiny cage.
And like a baby in a famine
You died of grief, not age.

Pat Morton

Legend Of The Lone Ranger

Dan Read was a ranger and chasing an outlaw,
He got isolated and left on his own,
He entered a cave, but his footing was unsure,
He stumbled and fell with a crackle of bone:
He didn't know how long unconscious he lay,
But came to in a terrible welter of pain.
He became aware of not being alone
When a strange voice was heard to say,
'I've reset your leg, so lie still, let it heal,
And you'll soon stand upon it again.'
It took him some days to be able to stand
And he looked round the cave he had found.
An Indian stood by with a feathered head-band.
Dan saw something shine on the ground;
It seemed he'd discovered and old silver mine,
He told his new friend, 'Half is yours, half is mine!'

The Indian christened him, 'Kemo Sabe,'
Which in his tongue meant trusty scout.
The Indian's name was Tonto, he did say
And he showed Ranger Dan the way out;
From a piece of black leather, Dan made a mask
And swore to uphold the law.
He practised his gun-draw and got really fast,
His trademarks would be known for sure:
Some silver he gathered and made into bullets
and searched for his trusty white horse.
With Tonto beside him, he went to fulfil it,
His oath for the law to enforce:
Their fame grew and grew throughout all the land,
No outlaw would stand in the way,
As the masked Lone Ranger came thundering by
As he yelled, 'Hi-yo Silver Away!'

Mick Nash

The Faceless Clock

The bedside table, the faceless clock
a silence only morning can imbue.

Pale light filters through the
fringe-edged curtains,
transforming dark into light
and sleep into consciousness.

The clink of a milk bottle,
someone clears his throat upon
the sombre, early morning street
before the incursion of familiar
footsteps is discernible.

Only the croak of the carrion crows
high in the canopy of the nearby oak trees
pervades the air whilst perched
like judge and jury upon another day of promise,
another dawn breaks with elementary calm
and the faceless clock needs only
to be put back one hour.

Thomas Liddle

SOMEWHERE ELSE

Where is your home?
Is it where you lay your head,
is it where your heart is,
is it where you are,
or is it somewhere else?

Where is your heart?
Is it where you are,
or is it with someone else?

Who is someone else?
Is he where you are,
or is he far away?
Somewhere else, waiting, hoping.

Keith Slatter

A Pictured Imagery With Memory

Many faces become placed
Into lasting reflections in memory
Like a lost understanding
In our desert of thought
We ourselves only remember
Just little fragments
From our pictured life
Sounds far passing
Yet shaped with form
The conversation
Adding one's interlude
Free from silence
Not a lonely void skull
A faded chorus
Muted in its shell
Hidden in that eternal
Passage of night
Buried out into the gardens
With solitude
An unending song
On life's storm-tossed sea
A signified image
In that found mountain
Of desolation
Written impressions
The sung poems
And lasting flowers
Carved from love's
Own heart.

Roger Thornton

ETERNAL BOND

Why me?
Why poetry?
Allows thought processes unleashed,
rolling in so fast,
to be penned to loved ones.
Dreams of days gone past.

Memories so precious,
memories best forgot,
hopes and aspirations,
captured on a page.
Written, unreservedly,
to an audience on a hidden stage.

What for?
For whom?
Part of my confusion,
needs to be released.
Unspoken, but sincerely meant,
feelings I have for you.

They told me that you died
but, I know that can't be true,
because I feel your presence,
you are always in my heart,
you are sitting close beside me.
No one can ever tear us apart.

Eve McGrath

SWEET MEMORIES

Sweet memories they were
Sitting under the sunset boughs
Drinking the summer breeze
Laughing under the sun's haziness.
Playing from morn till dusk
A tiring time for innocent limbs
Devoid of sadness, a happy time.

Samina Amjad

Just Two Lines

Just two lines between me and thee;
A mother and a father makes a family.
Two hearts wrapped in a solid foundation;
Between God and the nation.
How be it that the church bells toll;
Two simple heartbeats with only one role.
To be the one love I prayed for,
For so many years,
Is to hold your sweet love so close, so dear.
How do you explain life to all,
With one simple answer,
But not a call.
How do the years pass before memories are told:
Save it until others are old,
To let it unfold.

Pauline M Lowery

Fifty Comes And Goes

50 comes and 50 goes
What do we have to show?
A wrinkle here
A grey hair there
Or maybe not!

Wisdom comes
The 'Crone' emerges
Wiser than wise
She enters our psyche
When we are unaware.

She holds

Secrets in a wooden box
From years of ebbing and flowing
Papers lost in that sea of tranquillity
Waiting for time to elapse

Now ascending the stairs of life
Awakening her earthly life
A bud, a tree, a bird,
All brighter and more beautiful

Friends and Nature are her existence.

Barbara Glanfield

Beyond The Tamar

Beyond the banks of Tamar lies
A land of mystery and awe,
Of dark and dreadful histories,
Of cove and cavern, farm and moor.
There the Atlantic's mighty waves
Against the rugged cliffs are hurled,
And smugglers secreted in caves
Their contraband, hid from the world.
And wreckers lured to their doom,
Without remorse, vessels at sea,
While kith and kin, secure at home,
Prayed, 'Lord, from peril keep them free.'
Miners who searched for tin and gold
Hazarded in the depths their lives.
What endless stories could be told
Of daring, skill and enterprise.

And bold Trelawney, to his conscience true,
Still following, dauntless, what he saw as light,
Was in the Tower imprisoned and though he knew
Death might await him, would not yield to fright.

Cornwall, how justly proud thou art,
Not the least part of Britain, thou,
But from thy glorious past take heart
And make the future glorious too.

John W Garland

CONTENTMENT

Go across approaching valley
Past the trees on yonder hill
There you'll find a farmyard cottage
With a painted window sill
The yard it is all cobblestones
The roof is thatched with straw
The stove is polished, shining bright
The table timbers white and raw.

An old seat in the doorway
Holds a lady, grey and frail
The hens pecked at the speckled dust
Beside an upturned pail
Out in the yard, before the gate
Lies dog in summer's sun
Across, in field of swaying graze
Stands workhorse, now that work is done.

Each breath is one of freshness
With the scent of burning peat
Happiness, from fireside chat,
With canine friend across one's feet
Contentment is the essence
Of what one garners here
The lesson one of thankfulness
For each ongoing year.

D J Totten

A Carer's Morning Prayer

Grant endurance
to lovingly provide the constant care
needed as this day begins.

Grant guiding hands
to gently lead, as the way
grows dark and confused.

Grant patience
when vacant responses
evoke depression, replacing hope.

Grant tolerance
when, uncharacteristic intangible anger
inflicts undeserved wounds.

Grant understanding
when, no longer remembered,
wordlessly dismissed.

Grant forgiveness
when doubts of compassion
bring unbearable pain.

Grant peace
when this day is over . . . as this night begins.
Fortify and prepare me for tomorrow.

Polly Davies

An Invisible Being

You could be anybody at all
An enemy to see

At someone's beck and call
Or a person free to be

You could be short or tall
A he or a she

I'll never see you fall
'Cause you murdered me.

P Taylor

Passion, The Flow Of Life

Life is for living
And since you are already here,
You must as well live a full life.
Passion is the spirit of life.
As we know,
The spirit of life is love.
When the passion of life ebbs,
When you feel powerless
And desires hopelessly unfulfilled.
Fading passion, fading dreams?
Look inside yourself
Connect with your soul
Rediscover where passion comes from.
Passion comes from the heart
Passion comes from love
With the return of the spirit of passion
Life can never be stopped.
Passion, the healer of all desires
Brings you from darkness to the bright light.
Like a tree in the forest reaching out for the sun.
The flow of passion, the flow of infinite love,
The flow of infinite joy - the flow of life.

Akudeya

THE GOLDEN MILE

Children peeping over shoulders
the barker attempts
to entice customers
to his adults-only side-show.
Pedestrians push and shove
into an almost Asian bazaar
of rock neon
and fish and chips
under bridges of light.
Next along
girls from Mars
are on display.
Are they real?
C'mon, this is Blackpool!

Paul Wilkins

JOSEPHINE OF WALES

The human heart is a neon lamp post:
It is an empty glass case in the pouring rain:
It is a hand-hold in a huge crevasse
On the north face of the Eiger Mountain:
In short, I do not know what the human heart is,
Only that it is, wonderfully, there.

Edmund Saint George Mooney

Just For You

I know, I know what I would wish to be,
A little candle in your room;
I would shine, I would shine only,
I would shine just for you;
I would shine, I would shine only,
I would shine just for you.

I know, I know what I would wish to be,
A little bird outside your window;
I would sing, I would sing only,
I would sing just for you;
I would sing, I would sing only,
I would sing just for you.

I know, I know what I would wish to be,
A little flower in your garden;
I would bloom, I would bloom only,
I would bloom just for you;
I would bloom, I would bloom only,
I would bloom just for you.

Muriel Willa

Unemployment

A curse of our time
Is being on the dole,
The youth of today
Have committed no crime,
They don't deserve this role.

The future for them
Looks bleak indeed,
No prospects for the young,
All they seek
Is a right to work
And their young mouths to feed.

So you young folk out there,
I know the world
Seems bleak and cold,
But keep your spirits up,
You young ones,
Times they are a-changing
With everything computerised,
We'll do some rearranging.

J Pruden

GARDENING PLEASURE

At glancing out of my window
And after cutting grass,
My neighbour pruning rose trees,
So I blink for a second glance,
For looking at his profile,
I say, 'Oh, dearie me,'
The late gardening legend,
Mr Thrower, yes PT.
I rock back in my chair
To take a further look,
Again I get this profile
That's come straight out of a book.

M Bedford

September Song

Misty morning,
A spider's web
Sewn so finely with finest thread,
The morning sun is up above somewhere,
I see its rays breaking through the chill of the air.
Who tickled my face as through the gorse I walk?
Sorry Mr Spider,
Shh, why should I even talk?
A misty morning,
A spider's web,
A garland of jewels
Delicately laced
With fine silver thread.
Harvest time would
Once be shared by many,
Glad to be on these downs
After a week down the mine,
Now it's only me. Look
Blackberry stains on these ageing fingers of mine,
Hard earth beneath me, gorse now crowds my way,
As night falls, the stars above me,
They show me the way.
I go to greet the future with the image of the past,
God's beauty all around me,
The dew, the damp, one with creation.
Lord, when I'm too busy, please forgive me.

T Grant

A Feline To The Rescue

Come and comfort me, I am sad and so alone,
I need a companion to call my own,
A guide that is wise and tender to direct and supervise,
Who will offer, who will care? Who with me this life to share?
None avail or heed my plight as tearfully I bid all goodnight.
Oh cruelty, you do your best as ridiculous my life is a mess,
Unable to think or plan, those tyrants who destroyed my man.

I knew he had so many faults and never corrected all he ought,
Gunned down in cold blood by many crooks who stated he had fiddled so many books.
My lifestyle has changed from high to low, misdirected where to go,
Sad of heart and filled with woe, I need a shoulder to support as I plead so.
At last you came and I with open arms adore your generosity
And your charms, such a comfort and tenderness do you portray,
You promised me you will never, ever stray.

A feline to the rescue came and helped me wipe away the blame,
So calm and intelligent as all of assistance she aims to be,
So besotted with her I always agree, I have adopted my new found pet
As she is here with me and lingers yet, insisting I mention her in this so-called verse.
She is so cute and to make matters worse, she loves me.

R D Hiscoke

NEGLECT IN A SYSTEM

Britain is lacking in most everything
That a nation badly needs,
So it is time that they did something
For our potential to succeed.

Our health system is in tatters,
Where once it was the best.
It is through trying hard to privatise,
Which has caused all this unrest.

The public transport is a shambles,
Since cars and haulage have been used,
Here this was a grave mistake
When trail and tramways were abused.

Our education is a laughing stock
To other European nations,
We need teachers who are knowledgeable,
Who can change this situation.

Those three subjects are most vital
For a country to win success,
They should never be neglected
Or they will finish in a mess.

Lachlan Taylor

THE GHOST CHILD

The ghost child never eats, never sleeps,
Just cries and waits there
Begging for a measly quarter pound.
He often stops and wonders
Why his family were killed
In a war of which they had no cause.
People walk straight past him,
He's a sight there all used to see,
Hungry and cold he sits there
And now with a fatal disease,
Yet people still pass him by.
He's learnt to stop crying
As he knows no one shall ever come.
As he gets weaker and
His vision starts to fail,
He dreams of joining his family in the clouds,
Playing with his little sister
And being tucked into bed.
As he takes his last breath,
He leaves the world unnoticed.
Such a wasted little life
As he was only four.
His body lay for a few days,
Covered in rats and pests.
How could we let this happen? Why?
God bless poor little ghost child.

Peter Coulter

CLOISTERS

Evensong . . . the yard clock doth proclaim,
Sisters deep in silent conversation
Appear to float along
As if they themselves were all Gabriels . . .
Come to tell Mary the news.

The weighty prayer book
With its well-thumbed pages
All yellow and crackling, with use and age,
But Mother Superior says it was
Produced by monks in the sixteenth century
And insists we study our Latin.

The cloisters are buzzing with illicit gossip
Of crafty feasts of biscuits and apples.
Oh guilty were they that would sleep deeply on the
Crumbs of sin . . . and the core of all evils.
The sun gently warmed the moss-covered walls
And something in the air . . . yes, definitely.

Once more young blood,
Here she is, but a child
That has surrendered wholly to an ideal
And so the vows were taken.

All nuns have habits,
So had she.
Oh the shame for a stolen cigarette
Smoked secretly in the cloisters.
Twenty Hail Marys and two days silence,
But I think she was forgiven.

Sally Wyatt

THE TRUTH, THE WHOLE TRUTH AND THE BLOODY TRUTH

I wish I could wave a magic wand
To breach the tide of people's spite
Amongst the world where I belong,
Jealousies, discriminations at its height.

Their views, they should not be aired,
Their brush that taints the weak and poor,
Cause tongues so loose, nobody dared
Principles fired, a wicked allure.

What, moreover, I'd like to say
If only people'd stop, not stare
That as we move from day to day
Then I wouldn't really care.

To close nearer our goal is good
A little at a time must be our aim.
If it can be done it surely should
And it should be stressed it's not a game.

To move along this path is right
Our final aim must surely be
Although parameters are tight
A fairer place for you and me.

The final end-game scenario should stand
Where wise men and scholars would agree,
A proud and passionate movement in our land,
That change was there for all to see.

Paul Stokes

ENTHUSIAST

He was a mover
Refusing to stand still
Or do anything against his will.
He doesn't talk about
What he's actually going to do,
He just does the unpredictable
With nerve, cool and a little skill.

Champion of all that's fun to be had,
His favourite pastime being:
'You play Mum and I'll be Dad.'
But in this world of let's pretend,
The only real pleasure
Is the companionship of a true friend.

An eternal optimist,
Fighting for what you cannot buy or sell
And in his campaign for enjoyment
His watchwords are, 'Who's to tell?'

He doesn't worry about the future,
He doesn't regret the past,
He's just, 'A live now . . . together, enthusiast.'

Malcolm Peter Mansfield

THE ISLE OF MAY

Set like Charybdis athwart the Forth
Between the Bass and Carr Rocks, off Fife Ness,
It guards the sullen seaway from the north.
The tower revolves and semaphores ingress.
Pounding the Cleaver, lashing the Peregrine's Nest,
Spray blurs the light on Palpitation Brae.
Gales over Clett, the Middens and Whaup Rest
Proclaim another Scottish summer day.

MOD frigates pass, yawls from Arbroath.
Oil tankers ploughing up towards Blackness
Record the foaming depth charge. All are loath
To accept it's not three miles of barren wilderness,
But paradise. Kestrel, whimbrel, red-crowned firecrest,
Red-spotted bluethroat, greenshank, great grey
Shrike, marsh warbler, phalarope, golden plover nest
In the machair, the inheritors. Each day,

25,000 guillemots bask in the froth,
3,000 razor bills attack the sea's largess,
6,000 kittiwakes plunder the silt-rich broth,
12,000 puffins feed on sand eels. The waters effervesce,
Spindrift and roaring rocks press
Down upon shag, auk and eider duck. The spray
Refreshes fulmar and Arctic tern. conditions bless
The aboriginal denizens of the May.

Voles, seabirds, rabbits, seals and campion possess
God's little acre, reproductively. They spend their day
Heedless of passing boats, the destroyer's progress,
The sheer irrelevance of humanity.

Norman Bissett

FACELIFT

Waking after sleeping
now and then;
Facing up to starting
over again

Searching with a will
for reasons - why?
Need to carry on still,
cave in gracefully

Bear it, come what may,
the hardest choices
sure to have their way
with us

Dawn gathering pace,
putting on a face

R N Taber

Adjectives And Verbs

A poem has the power to paint a picture with punctuation and words.
A seething sea of adjectives faces us.
A coloured rainbow arches overhead with vibrant verbs.
The grandeur of a pebble beach which the ceaseless waters pound,
Rocks, cliffs and inlets, the sea scoured, stark reality of nouns.
Stops and commas in the distance fly; the merest dots.
With flocks of seabirds; gulls and gannets and guillemots.
As they dip and dive,
To ride over the wind-blasted cliff tops,
A question mark is the stark, wind-bent tree,
On the headland seemingly writhing in agony.
Apostrophes, wind-torn leaves,
Scattered by the brisk breeze.
Whilst in the shelter of the park,
Stretches upwards, a stark exclamation mark,
Of an Italian cypress tree.
In mockery to the wind,
Whose belligerent vowels rise in tormented howls,
As the demented air screams and runs amok.
The consonants, rippling grasses,
Dotted and dashed with wild flowers,
All must contrive to survive,
These wind-plagued hours.
So ends the picture tale,
Of an early autumn gale.
Just words, dots and dashes,
But see how they prevail.

Jonathan Pegg

REFLECTIVE POOLS

I sit under an apple tree
waiting
for an apple to drop.

(Gravitas in gravity.)

I walk up a path
to the temple
never to walk back again.

The sounds of the traffic
cease, the shouts
and screams of people
are silent.

The birds welcome the dawn,
their wings in flight
freeing my mind.

I count each hour
pass by longing
for the day we can share
our days of love again.

When the apple drops
I shall not be here
to catch what was never there.

(Gravity in gravitas.)

The real into the unreal
is a circular speculation.

The unspoken is
the ecstasy of being.

Michael Alan Fenton

The Sun Shines On The Holy Land

The sun rose,
pushing through the darkness
as if it were a child struggling to be born.
Spreading its golden light before it.
Trumpeting hope.

For, if it had a voice
surely that voice would shout, ‘Look, look at me,
I bring hope . . .’
But the sun does not have a voice,
it does not bring hope,
just another hot day in Hell . . .

Valerie McKinley

THE WAR CRIMINAL

When the redcoats
Bearing muzzle-loaded hounds
Dropped all indictments,
The war criminal felt slighted.

So much for those ravaged sheep
And defiled chickens, he thought.
Died ecstatic, I suppose,
Praising my hallowed name.

The fox was
Elastic enough to
Adapt to changing circumstances

And was soon found
Dead at the side of the road,
Its dash to
Outrun fast traffic having
Ended in condemnatory paragraphs
In the local press
And a total ban on cars from
Certain stretches of country roads.

Peter Asher

ARE WE ALWAYS THINKING?

Are we always thinking,
Or is thinking only achieved by the more mature and upper classes?
Thinking about thinking
Is like listening about listening,
Is like hearing about hearing,
Is like learning about learning,
But it is not.

You can create evidence about when one is talking,
But can you create evidence to prove one was thinking?
Do you only think when you feel like it,
Or do you always think,
Whether it be consciously or subconsciously,
I think we always think,
Or do I?

Do I think we always think,
Do I think,
What is 'to think'?
To process things in the mind,
Is life constantly being processed in the mind,
Is life constantly being 'thinked about,'
What is life . . ?

Daniel C Wright

The Seagull

(After Anton Chekhov)

'If I could give you these arms
To flow on sailed glides,
With unblinking eye to catch myself
Rooted to this crag. The tide's
Teasing froth in climbing calms
Cling then self-consuming subsides.
Falling far short of your nestled shelf
Where stealth from flight resides
And no human longing harms.'

The bird is thrown onto the lawn,
Symbol of innocence, driftwood
From the dry lake the lover swims.
'Words, words, words,' but none could
Explain his misplaced passion:
With Freudian inheritance, he misunderstood
Love for another while the past disarms
Every advance that he would
Make. A shot brings the curtain down.

Alexander Cuthbert

(SWEEP) SHADOW

Months after Sweep died, the search began
To locate a rare Blue-Roan and tan.
I couldn't; so came Blue-Roan number three.
(Sweep) Shadow was what her name would be.

We needed to fill the empty space
With another Cocker's friendly face.
Some may think that one dog should do,
But one's only half as good as two.

Of course, she's delightful as puppies are,
And our own special scintillating star,
Who seems to have a clever streak,
Learning her name within one week.

Biting feet is her main misdemeanour,
Affording her a great deal of pleasure.
A firm 'no' from me and she answered back,
So I had to use a different tack.

A whistle brought a positive result,
So I don't think it'll be too difficult
To get her to conform to what we desire,
Just consistency and patience we'll require.

Ina J Harrington

THE THICK PLOTTENS

Guy Fawkes
Secret talks
Shadowy figures
Fingers on triggers

Whispers louder
Lethal gunpowder
Ready to blow
In cellars below

Heavy footfall
Skin starts to crawl
Parliament's best
Soldiers arrest

Defendant charged
Stories enlarged
The guilty hung high
Ha! What a guy!

Robert Chiswick

DISTORTION

Through distorted eyes
We see a distorted world
With distorted people.

Through distorted hearing
We hear distorted music
With distorted sound.

Through distorted speech
We speak a distorted language
With distorted meanings.

Through distorted smells
We smell a distorted aroma
With a distorted scent.

Camilla Davidge

PLANNING PERMISSION GRANTED . . .

Dust from the falling house
Covers leaves and flowers.
A thin film turning
High summer to autumn.
Slowly it falls, pushed
By the yellow claw,
Arm turning and bowing
To nudge another wall
Down, into a red brick cloud.
Tall chimneys crash,
Wave farewell to the
Watching, silent garden.

Trees around the house
Whisper as each wing falls,
Protecting the disturbed,
Hiding their memories
In encircling arms.
Tall green sentinels
Guarding secrets from the past.

Other walls will grow
To fill the void
Within the trees
And other hands will touch
The bark, wondering
Who had gone before?
Sit within the welcome shade.
Brush away cobwebs of the past,
Pretend that ghostly fingers are
Fronds of feathery grass.
Soft voices just murmurs
Of a summer's breeze.

Sheila Seabourne

A Moon's View Of Earth

Suspended sphere,
In that vast ocean of the celestial heavens,
Like a blue and white marble,
Thrust at the hands of a child,
Randomly to roll upon the playground of space,

You came to rest,
In the position that now contains you,
Over eons I have watched,
As you were moulded and shaped,
When fate decreed a new creation,

Through the cosmic dust,
That pervades the atmosphere,
Bombardment from comet and asteroid sought you,
I too bear witness,
To the hostile activity of the universe,

Scars and craters,
Reign upon my surface also,
We were separated at birth,
In the great creation,
Forged from atoms, molecules and gases,

I watch from afar,
How beautiful you are,
A sapphire jewel in the casket of the heavens,
A planet amongst stars,
And I, a battered reminder,

This our galaxy, the Milky Way,
Contains us within invisible boundaries,
You a fragile orb in this hostile universe,
A part of some unique blueprint,
Of which the Architect only holds the design.

Ann G Wallace

My Cure

I was away in a surreal world
Enduring a new life, beginning to find me,
My past was behind me.
Then, a view on the wall beside me,
The past hurt me so much,
In truth it destroyed me,
But also helped establish me
Into what I am today.

Once in this surreal world
I was being myself,
Socialising through new technology.
Who would have imagined
It would be the rebirth of me?
That was the day I found my cure,
From that moment, I was sure.

Our paths had already crossed,
The chemistry unknown,
A new rapport constructed
And I set on a pilgrimage of curiosity.
I'll always remember that day, lucky day, my birthday.

I saw him from a distance,
Hiding and ambling around.
Little did he know
That was the day he became found.

He wore the colour black,
There was no going back.
I had found my cure,
A new light in my life
Who was there for me, shining bright.

Although my past still has depressive holds on me,
I'm happy knowing that
Nothing has ever felt so right
Within me, my faith is back,
Safe and alright.

Bethan Groves

THE WIND

Have you seen the wind blow?
Neither you or I, but watch the corn bend its head
To let the wind go by.
Have you seen the wind blow?
Neither you or I, but watch the waves hit the shore
To let the wind go by.
This miracle God has planned,
Only he sees the wind go by the wind.

Roland Torn

VILLAGE GREEN

All around the village green
The breath of real England.
Like a voice hoping and
Giving your light,
Like a pub, oh so joyful,
It smiles and sings.
A breath of old England
My song sings.
I sing a song of happiness,
I want all the world to feel
Gladness in our hearts,
The happiness I feel
Around the village green
Love is my friend,
I sing a song of happiness,
The love I feel.

Robert Peckham

A DEATH OF SORTS

I was born to die,
To live again in the wind
To breath life through motionless trees
To dance with the waves of the sea
And gently brush each cheek with a kiss.

So only with your eyes, you see but a still shell
A frame without a picture
A locked door with no key
A hollow well.

Yet now, feel that I am everywhere
Walking beside you
Dancing behind you
Running in front of you
Always with you
Undiminishing
Forever green.

Sarah A O'Leary

In The Corner, Under The Table

I lived my life in the corner
Watched everyone pass me by,
I hid from what I knew was true
And the fright of their fury.

I wish I could have left it all
Behind in the distance,
I wish that time and I
Could live side by side.

Around the edge there seems
A heavy burden hanging,
And in the dust is written
A lie from the past.

Pulling down from heart below
And listening ever long,
From places not unknown
Comes a bitter cry, alone.

April Cridland

LONG EXPECTED

Perhaps this is it, a morning long expected, yearned for turning point,
accomplishment, completion of the whole, the simple key
revealing everything - or clinging to an obstinate illusion
return to some half-suspected self-deception, a silently abiding
like the moon, even in first sunlight, pendant asymmetric
marble, sensual, unsmiling; more beautiful for that.
I view her through sleepy eyes, air slow and sticky with
the film of night that lingers on the skin. O quietly despairing!
Thing so easily fall apart, small joys so blithely dissipated
that only cautiously I draw the curtains back, inserting
an irreversible conclusion or beginning
and hesitate at the touch of light with a kind of fear.
Look, the stars have gone out; all night they burned
in their stellar spaces, all night they sang. Childlike,
I wonder now where they are, hidden existence, the silent
sigh of a candle flame.

The garden holds some lingering shreds of desolation
that dawn revealed as though reluctant to release its early
acquisition. Silently, so silently it sits,
I could believe it was a living creature, curled
unwaking at my feet; though I hear the long rattle
of a train crossing the viaduct and a crow voicing
its broken orison. What is my prayer? What is the destiny
of little things that rest in the stillness, waiting for release?
Water standing limpid in a glass, bending light,
could be a metaphor, plain image of the way it should be,
the how and what, the promise, the unsuspected ecstasy
of knowing the moment to be filled, this day, this morning,
every morning, long expected.

Barry Conaway

The Tenement Parade

In the thin mustard gas night
an old man makes his way
through the cold crowds

and the snow.
Age has wasted his flesh
and laid bare his bones

to the cold years.
Around him Christmas lights
glow rainbow bright,

like silent fireworks frozen.
Fireflies, rooted in concrete,
stutter vertically on

and beckon him back
to the tenement parade.
Entering the black cave

he climbs the stairs to his home.
One bar struggles amberly
to disperse the chill.

Fully dressed he climbs into bed,
and in a foetal cuddle
closes his eyes on the world.

David Morgan

THE MOURNE PRINCESS

This lovely maid was out one day
Some primroses to pick, her hair
Was black and shoulder length and
A lovely friendly smile

The Prince of Mourne he came along
Upon his great white horse
And saw this girl of beauty, he
Dismounted right away

'Good morning,' he politely said
And gently raised his hat, he
Was liked by all his tenants and
A noble-man he was. The girl was
Only eighteen years, the Prince
Was two years more

He saw she wore a chain of gold
A pendant round her neck
Most kindly he did ask her if
She knew where from it came
'My mother, she gave it to me when
I became eighteen.'

He asked her for to take him home
And meet her mother too, to this she gave
Consent to go and introduced the prince

'This necklace that she sweetly wore
Was in the wooden basket that was left outside
My door, when she was one or two days old'
The Prince, he said, 'Do you know Ma'am,
This is my uncle's child and I have found
A cousin and my bride to be as well.'

He took her to the castle where they were wed
She was the royal princess
That he met that lucky morn.

Patrick M Crory

THE CHRISTENING

My baby was held by the vicar
wrapped snugly inside a white gown.
Her candle was starting to flicker
and people beginning to frown.
'I'm waiting to christen your daughter.
Her relatives fill every pew.
Before I can sprinkle the water
shall I give her one name or two?'
I thought, it's not Wilhelmina,
a name which is very obscure.
Nicola, Carlotta and Gina
are foreign, so think up some more.
Her grandmother's name is Amelia
and I'm called Betty or Bess.
My hubby likes Denise and Delia,
His mother wants Trudy or Tess.
The baby is starting to whimper;
the vicar will think I'm insane.
My father has got such a temper
and wouldn't go through this again.
I think we considered Diana
and thought about Barbara-Anne.
We firmly rejected Susanna,
Clarissa, Joanna and Pam.
Our name for a boy would be Percy
but I had a beautiful girl.
The curate likes Faith, Hope or Mercy
And Uncle, Patricia or Pearl.
If something so odd is selected
this baby is called it for life.
I can't have the ones we rejected,
I don't want to cause any strife.

I whispered, 'I'm rather a blockhead
and the baby is not very plain,
but please make a cross on her forehead
and christen her Agatha Jane.'

Nancy Reeves

MOSHAV

The young Irish teacher on the Moshav, got
really friendly with the farmer. Word was
she raised more than just his language awareness, but

she worked hard and helped talk away his
long desert night's guard duty, dutifully listening
and collocating the opposition. She

showed him glimpses of Ireland, lush and wet
and green and in return he showed her how to
strip his M16. In fact, by the time she left,

she was fluent. She could do it in the dark,
faster than him and he was impressed. But
as he said, he was only the farmer.

Afterwards, they back-chained a cigarette together and
smelling of gun oil and American tobacco, looked out
into the desert, their red dots brazenly beating the stress.

John Kay

Home Coming

The house is in darkness.
He switches on the lights
    and moves slowly
    from room to room.

She is here on every chair,
by every door.
She touches each
    plate, dish and glass
    that he holds.
There is a silence everywhere.

As long as he lives there
    so will she.
When he leaves
    they will go together.

Kinsman Clive

The Depth Of Dark Despair

Deep in the dark bowels of the Earth
Manly bodies saturated with sweat from their labours
In tight confined spaces
Shovels and picks in sequential rhythm
With breathlessness of the yielder
Their fruits conveyed from the mineral source
To the mouth of the seam
The mixture of underground gases
Reaching a final crescendo
A crematorium in the pits of Hell
For the majority of its occupants
The few spared blindly smell their way
Over rubble using springs to quench thirsts
Day after day clawing a path to freedom
Finding the path blocked
Frantically digging their nails into concrete
Left to rot in the depths of dark despair.

Phil Clayton

THE DEATH OF A CHAMELEON

Once rainbow eyes that wheeled in bright malevolence
Are closed in bulging slits
And dusty blood now streaks
The lurid, green lizard skin.

The tight tail that hung in coiled benevolence
Around the scrap of pepper tree,
Is flat and bent and very dead
For this little world and God to see.

My cat now sulks behind a curtained valance
Brooding over a poisoned tongue;
Another minor African death
About which no song is sung.

S M Hogsden

The Kiss Of The Well-Honed Steel

She feels no pain
just the release
as the blade caresses her flesh,
and she savours the kiss
of the well-honed steel,
as the flow of blood
washes her clean,
calming her, giving her the peace
she craves, releasing her from the pent up fury
that smothers her
and setting her free.

And in that desperate moment
of the recognised loss of her childhood
she remembers the blossoming time of her future.

No longer a girl, not quite a woman
but she feels like a woman feels
and only women bleed.

The well-honed steel sings in her hand
and again makes love to her flesh,
desecrating her soul.

And all the time the need,
the longing for someone to hear
the silence of her torment,
the need that is hers to own,
the need to be free,
to face the world and shout,
'I'm here world, I'm still here,
and I'm still me.'

Alexander K Stubbs

Is Anyone Out There?

They visit us from worlds afar, arriving in spaceships, not in a car,
Bringing new technologies for us Earthlings, expanding our brains, giving us wings,
From beginnings of time the signs were there, UFOs, that's too absurd,
I'm telling you this I think it's true, look around, it's up to you.

Is it science, or military tests, do your eyes deceive, or is it jest?
Yet from the past the future comes, the government the country runs,
Tell the truth no one believes, a crackpot, fool, is what they see,
The proof we need is hard to find, is it fact, or in the mind?

Ray Stuart

God Bless You

'God bless you,' said the rich man
with so little thought
he has much wealth and power
much more than he ought.
His mind is taken over
with thoughts of goods and store
his greed is so demanding
he must get more and more.

'God bless you,' said the poor man
he meant it as a prayer
he stood shaking in a doorway
his bones were almost bare.
He had nothing else to offer
nothing else to give
he had no wealth or power
or even a place to live.

Which of these words are priceless
which would you prefer to keep
the thoughtless words of the rich man
or those said with feelings deep?

W T Ahern

THE CUCKOO

I heard the cuckoo singing
One early summer morn
His tone was full of music
As he heralded the dawn.
When he sang a happy note
Fell from his merry throat
I listened with enchantment
To the message that he brought.

I heard the cuckoo singing
When came the close of day
Still rang that note of sweetness
Of his, happy roundelay.
But, the message that he brought me
So early in the morn
Lived with me forever
When the cuckoo bird had flown.

Mary Ferguson

So Well Recited

Each day I know you will return, the only true certainty of life.
Did you melt into the mountains at the end of the day
Fold into the fields or slip into the sea?
I wonder, did you cheekily peep from behind a lathered nimbus before your evanescence?
All this in preparation for your next recital.
Undoubtedly your final flaunt would be of blended tones.
For now, I await the dawning day to see your emergence from beneath.
A performance so well recited.
Anticipated excitement stirs within me as you puncture the horizon.
A stream of liquid gold seeps through, brightening the forenoon.
Your leisurely rise this fine day, a performance so well recited.

Mary Morley

PHOTO ALBUM

Pouring over old photos brings the opportunity
to access the past.
Are memories true reflections of events
or embellished to suit nostalgic needs?
How often do we say, Oh I remember that day well?
Conflict with other family members whose recollections
bear no resemblance to one's own.
The camera never lies, does it?
Captured on celluloid a personal interpretation
of light, shade and tone: give twenty people the
same subject and twenty different pictures materialise.

Are we to assume from this diversity of 'product'
that there is no truth? Other than our personal
ideas on how we would like the audience to view
our achievements. Technology forges ever onward,
heedless to any notion of restraint. progress
confined within a box: the moment the shutter
closes, life becomes a catalogue.
We are a nation obsessed with story telling on
a grandiose scale wanting our children to be
aware of how trendy, outrageous or
truly rounded we were.

Photographs help to identify what we looked
like and how life appeared to be. Is this sense
of identity sufficient to accurately portray events
of great importance? Arguably so.

'Reminiscence therapy' isn't that what it is called?
Personally, smells and sounds are more evocative
of past times:- photographs can act as a catalyst
to unlock timeless memories; to provide the complete
picture - without them would we remember anything
so clearly?

Sarah Allison

THE I AM

I am the hedgehog that you come across, frantically
collecting things from beneath the tall blades.
I am the sniper outside your bedroom window
I am the driver who went slightly too fast but never crashed
I am the champion of the tallest peaks and greatest leaps
I am the apple collector in the forests across the world
searching for just enough to break even
I am the deejay on your radio, mixing records for all to enjoy
I am the commander of a great fleet of men, who will move out,
at the push of a button.

I am the infinity of the universe
I am the calmness of the sky
I am the purple twilight with all
I am the grey, the family logo.

I am the victor in all battles
I am the one who restored peace to many nations
ruled by dictatorship
I am the noble plumber who tried his best
I am the one who opened the path to enlightenment
through mischief
I am the trainer who will go to the extreme
for the best of the team.

I am the circles, crosses, triangles and squares
I am the letters and numbers, the left and right
I am the interconnectivity to another world
I am the original system designed to amaze
and distort reality.

Lynsey Stopforth

The Path Of Life

He gave us life.
Our right to choose
Which way we tread our path.
He gave us evil, born of sin.
A way to show our wrath.
Some are born to hate,
Will they take the righteous path?
Or will it be too late?
So make your choice
And don't look back.
Courage never lack,
For life is such a tiny house.
Furnish it with love.

J P Cook

Wedded Bliss

Wearisome worries engulf my mind
Some trite and trivial
As I try to swim into the unconscious
Then I remember that nothing matters
Except that I lie here with you
In sombre sleep
Surrounded by the silence of the night
Knowing that you love me.

Carmel Lynch

THE DYING GAUL

There the dying Gaul doth lie
Cold marble yet alive
He did not ask the reason why
Or flee thus to survive.

He hears no more the victor's hail
Nor feels the iron thrust
No sorrow now he knows at all
Nor fear, nor pain, nor lust.

The flesh is turned to marble
His head bowed to his breast
Forever there on the Capitoline Hill
Will his brave memory rest.

Yet lives on his spirit brave
While Empires rise and fall
And peoples that were once enslaved
Survived to tell his tale.

From the tragedy of man's dark past
Emerges classic art
Unimagined when the die was cast
Again fate played its part.

And as the silent crowds pass by
That superbly sculptured form
They may reflect how works of art
From brutal acts are born.

C O Burnell

WINTER IN CONCERT

Wrapped in home comforts
protection from winter's ice storm
hibernate,
Thawed together
Winter's woven garden lawn.
Hearts of oak for each other
True lover's knot
Sharing synchronous dreams
with future fantasies to plot.
Creating illusions
We've been cast in starring roles
together, we are co-producing
a romantic glamorous fantasy,
rekindling our souls
over candlelight evening song.
With heavy fall of snow outside
praying for winter to prolong.
Our passion, we cannot hide.

Peter A Wilde

THE TWO WORLDS OF THE SUN

The sun rises high above,
Into the morning sky
Like a swift golden angel,
With his precious golden wings
To bow down to our father God

The sun has risen,
Into the mighty ocean sky
Like a mighty boat of gold,
With rich powerful oars
Sailing from ocean to ocean
Dreaming never to be shipwrecked at all

On the same day you see this golden angel
With precious golden wings
Sinking like a boat of gold,
With rich powerful oars
Battling from ocean to ocean,
Yet, fading away into the evening sky
Dreaming to return for another adventure soon.

Niresha Umaichelvam (10)

DOUBLE DELIGHT

To have a tiny being
A replica of one's own
Is such a wonderful thing in life
The best you've ever known
But to be given two such tiny beings
Must mean such joy and pride
Two pretty little faces
Each laying side by side
Four tiny hands, four tiny feet
Soft as soft can be
Two downy heads, two button noses
There for all to see
Four rosy cheeks, two dimpled chins
Blooming, just like petals
Four velvet ears, four starry eyes
On which the eyelid settles
Two rosebud lips to smile at you
And to kiss goodnight
God surely must have blessed you
To have given such double delight.

Caroline Kelsey

PEOPLE

Have you ever noticed
The way people talk,
Say things they don't mean?

The way they act towards you
Also how it seems that you are the one giving
A group becomes separate then one person.

The past is nothing but a tool
That goes forwards or backwards,
The people you knew are now on solid ground.
The question is where do you stand?

Ise Obomhense

ATTENTION

You say you need no
attention
That's sad
Because attention means
care
consideration.

My soul weeps
for you
when you say
abstract
nothings
like that.

Do you feel you're not
worthy of care,
consideration
Are your emotions
so far
cut?

Christina C Simpson

ALMOST HOME

I travel the road of life with sorrow in my eyes and
pain in my heart avoiding the obstacles that the world
throws at me avoiding the obstacles of sin.

I travel the road of life although sometimes I stop and
rest at the side of the road, I sit and look around
I am alone.

I travel the road of life, I walk and slip and fall
all I can do is carry on walking towards home,
I have to keep going without giving up.
I am almost home.

C J Walls

EASY RADIO

Radio pumping out
Thoughts falling around
A break in a tune
What is it I'm doing,
Am I sad or lonely with no one here
But my window and me

Hard to find people new
Where have they gone?
Radio thumping again
Pop-rock
To hip-hopping shock
How simple they
Make life seem

E A Triggs

NOT A SAD PHOTO-PLAY

Fiona knew how she might be broken by sadness,
Weakened by woe, frozen by sorrow
And remembered as being alien to gladness -
For there seemed to be no tomorrow.

Jonathon was dead, prime life bespoken by ill-luck
Unforeseen and thought to be not rife -
Yet it had struck him down, his plans unstuck
With failure and illness - he and his wife.

The last scene in the film was of a hill at sunrise.
Fiona and Jonathon were dwarfed -
It seemed to imply - by Nature's near-eternal guise.
Sheila and Jack, graceless, could have laughed
At such an interpretation at another time
But he was aware, love conquered all
And she believed love sustained all in condition prime
Beyond Nature's most restrictive call.

For Sheila was hard of hearing and had faulty speech
And poor Jack had defective eyesight.
But Sheila painted pictures vivid with colour, each
Showing a new world live with light
And Jack could sing baritone songs that melted the heart
And brought the soul, trembling, into play -
So that it seemed - between them - Nature was only a part
Of what everyone is each day.
Their stories traced misfortune, woe, sorrow and despair
In real life, not a sad photo-play -
And also traced courage and a will to be - like a dare -
Themselves, as each of us in the way
We travel along.

S V Batten

Maria Rua

Lapping tides of emotion, embrace her surreal surface,
The sun caresses upon her silver tears,
An angelic pale complexion, that confiscates time,
An enchanting spell of the heart spun, a legacy of love in rhyme.

Changing seasons awash with dapple strokes, a radiant beauty divine,
A human canvas of texture, a precious fusion intertwined,
Calming new dawning, a tranquil serenity,
Her mothering presence provides the sustenance of destiny.

Jade optical vision, the eyes and sight of her soul,
A vivid, rich horizon that will glisten the most, darkest goal,
An illumine lady, of versatile wisdom and gracious maturity,
A complicated elegance, that weeps for lasting security.

She stimulates fantasies, her hidden depths never revealed,
A shy timid nature, mysterious secrets concealed,
An inner harmony, so near to self peace,
An exile of her own conscience, pending final release.

A ray of hope eternally smiles on her rugged finesse,
A scenic splendour, who is heavenly blessed,
She has unlocked passions, and set sensitive spirits free,
She is the personification of beauty, the wild terrain of Red Marie . . .

Leon O'Doherty

PHENOMENOLOGY

Unified, then the dichotomy of specification
Focused on, the dichotomy grows
And then seems like nothing beside the void
Collective, planar, constructive always
Causing the focus on the void . . .

Michael Courtney Soper

But Where?

Will we walk through the valley
In the sense of, come where
To see, in the midst, of the garden, so fair.
There, as in tender, an ever behold,
The colours so fine, as they turn so to gold.
Each colour enhancing,
To my eyes, they are glancing.
I cannot believe, that the story's, not told
Blues all around, in the cause, of all sound,
With yellows, but creeping, enfold
Such beauty and grace, will give of their space.
To assemble in far, distant shore,
Does seem, like it's far,
Beyond distant star.
As the dewdrops, of show, their embrace,
It seems, in a dream, all as labelled, between,
The black note, of white, is begun,
And where, came the rain
To the clouds, their remain,
Are in keeping, the beams of, the sun,
I'll gather, the colours, as one turns to one,
Beginning the pinks, with the reds,
All cosy and warm, to assemble, not harm.
As they cluster, throughout, o'er the beds,
The green to be seen, what're, can it mean,
Like the emerald, all haggard, and torn,
Outstanding behold, in the sprinkling, of gold,
Rainbow's end, at beginning, of morn.

Hugh Campbell

Food Of Life

Golden is the cry of the swaying corn,
in a sun-blessed Heaven of our given land.

Like our roots in the valley of our birth
the crop digs down in search of goodness,
from the earth.

For all time, throughout the passing years,
from Celtic times to present days,
the food of life has grown this way.

David Bilsborrow

A Smile

The stranger who
Walked towards me, was
Looking sad and blue,
I saw her first
And wondered how
Her face could be so rue.
I thought perhaps she'd
Had bad news, or
Maybe lost her purse
But since I didn't
Know these things
To comment I was averse
So I smiled at her
As I walked along
Giving her all my best
And as she looked
And came my way
With eyes so wide and new,
She smiled at me,
Her face lit up
Gone were the lines so blue
Her face once rue was shining true
It made my day to see her smile
As I went on my way.

Ruth Toombes

SALTMARSH

Sea lavender grows
In purple profusion
And marran grass
Sighs in the wind
Sea birds fly
Against the sky
Wheel and cry
And the sea sprays up on the strand.

So quickly the tide
Flows up to the land
Soon all will be
Covered and gone
And swishing and crashing
The waves will abound
Making a rushing beating sound
As all the beach is drowned.

Maureen Oglesby

What Is Love?

My uncle had an antique clock
    (It forecast weather too!)
A lady with a parasol came out
    dark clouds to mock
Assuring of a nice warm day
    each morn at 8 o'clock

Contrary-wise her partner would
    venture out one day
In muffler and an overcoat to
    warm inclemency.
We children thought it funny,
    they never both appeared
And guess that they had quarrelled
    very badly we averred.

Knew nothing of the bond they had
    or what their action moved,
Why always she had sunshine and he
    was always cold;
Nor that the bond between them
    was so strong as action proved,
Or what it was that bound them
    and such a power moved.

It was not love; a metal bar that
    answered cold or heat,
Enough to urge the lady out
    or activate her spouse
And send him wrapped for winter
    from the little wooden house.
The pressure of the temperature met
    all the puppets need

We marvel at our neighbours, our
friends, ourselves indeed
And wonder what the magic is
controls our human need!

E Norman

POET AND WRITER

I will come to you again my love.
You have warmed my heart and dried my tears.
You have always been near.
Whispered kind words to comfort
And to cheer.
Surprises pleasant as can be you brought.
Out of the blue
You gave me wings to fly
To lands I only dreamed about
New friends also and crowds for company.
I saw my name in lights and in print,
Poet and writer
Yet I go away again
Leaving you and doing all I can
So I may live
When my life is over
How would I be remembered?
Poet and writer?
Or just a woman who gave you
Very little time?

Hannah Yaawusuah Adjepong

A SLEEPING CITY

Stand on the bridge in the pale of the morn,
Look at the sleeping city,
Grey light
Tugging at dawn.

The buildings are outlined,
More solid and strong
In this azure black night,
Tinged with red of the morn.

Motionless, waiting for dawn to break through,
Watching in flight
As again they will die
When the world sheds its light.

Pamela Rollin

CEMENT CITY

Concrete pillars, concrete walls, concrete stairways, concrete floors,
Concrete car parks, concrete roads, concrete buildings,
Festooned with glass chrome surroundings.
A hideous mass, concrete workers, concrete jobs,
Locked in their prisons of concrete and glass,
No time to watch the world go by.
No time to watch the changing sky.
Towering towers so cold and still,
Nothing of beauty to break this scene,
Perhaps a pot of flowers, sometimes seen.
Tortured skyline, demented traffic streaming by,
Where is the beauty, we once had,
Just an occasional tree that looks so tired.
Move with the times we are told,
But all this just leaves me cold.
How I yearn for green fields, of forests,
Of those elegant beautiful trees.
Of rivers and hillsides and valleys and downs,
I ache to see mountain peaks shrouded in mist.
The dawn chorus of birds
And to feel the sun's kiss.
All this given up for power and greed,
These monsters of concrete we really don't need.
Just memories now, this beauty we had,
Knock a hole in this concrete,
Plant flowers galore,
Let the beauty of nature fill the cities once more.

Tom Usher

First Love

First love travels through Time
A constant companion, silent,
Invisible, unmentioned, locked in,
Crystallised forever in the mind.
Protected as fine China in a cabinet, rarely looked at but always there.

How beautiful he was.
His black hair, olive skin.
The flash of humour, the affectionate teasing,
His smile unsullied by sadness.
Open, uncluttered by responsibility.
Uncomplicated by doubt, carefree in Youth's optimism.

How precious is the remembering
Carefree joy which has never faded.
It remains in memory's room
Untainted perfection
Untrammelled by life's lottery of fortune.
Like Binyon's soldiers,
Always young, always handsome
Forever smiling as in a photograph.

Helena Pell

Before The Truce

Nine o'clock on a bright summer's morning
two whom never bothered to count the dead;
hurried through Red Cow Lane while hopping
a hired out handcart across the cobblestones.

They had travelled 300 bloody centuries
to put right things left. The Province was ruled by
a minority of stern faced bigots. The loquacious kind
happy around the table shuffling their bloodstained hands.

The boys stopped outside number 12 Red Cow Lane
and tipped up the handcart. Brennan, as stiff as
a bag of coal, slid onto the pavement outside the door.
The brass doorknocker received ill treatment and a

young girl answered the violence as her large eyeballs
turned to onions. She screamed. Bastards, rotten bastards.
They turned away, hopping the empty handcart out of the lane.
The rooftop sparrows scattered and darkened the sunlit morning.

Francis Hughes

DON'T TELL ANYONE BUT . . .

It's raining hard and I'm inside,
It's been practising all night long.
I'm sorry for the folk who must go out,
But listen to my joyous song.

I love the blatter on the windowpane,
And the gurgling under the eaves.
I'm glad I'm not a postman, but
Who on earth believes
That walking in a gale-force wind
Is really that much fun?
It's surely better to be snug and warm,
And wait for the glint of the sun.

I'm sorry for the men who go to sea,
And the ones who work on the roads,
I'm sorry for the women pushing prams,
And for coalmen sagging under loads.
I'm sorry for the kids who walk to school
(I'm sure there's one or two still)
I'm sorry for the telephone engineers
Mending lines at the top of the hill.

But I rejoice when a storm begins
And Thor and his minions ride,
I love it when I find, to my delight,
It's raining hard - and I'm inside.

D M Anderson

ELDERLY JOYS

A pattering at the window - there I see
A few bright drops, then rivulets of rain.
I leave my book. I feel an urge to flee,
To dash out, splash out, be a child again!
Out in the downpour under dripping trees
I walk among the rain-evicted worms,
Squelching in mud and the late autumn leaves,
Viewing the landscape's rain-bemisted forms,
Then, shiv'ring, homewards I turn once more,
Miserably cold and wet to the skin.
The cat is waiting for me at the door
And is quite overjoyed to be let in.
Dry clothes, the fire, the cat upon my lap,
Hot tea, good book - of all joys these are top!

V M Archer

LONELINESS

How
can one be so lonely,
with many friends about? But it is true.
For though the sun shines brightly, warmly down,
the days are permanently dark and icy cold.
Such loneliness can leave an aching void within.
A darkness of the mind, which will not part, as clouds might do,
to let a gleam - the merest mote - of light or warmth through to the soul,
slowly becomes a stygian blackness darker by far
than that which can be found inside the deepest pit.
And so with forced good cheer and empty smile,
the lonely one plods blindly on.
Clutching desperately to the white stick of death to guide him
on his way towards the welcome haven of unending rest.
Where finally, he will catch up and join again,
with those dear ones who went ahead
so he will be,
no more,
alone.

D G W Garde

MRS JONES

So you think you are better
Than us in every way
Because your house is bigger
Or the phrases that you say.
Your bank account is healthy
And your job is just fine
A huge car sits in your drive
'Yes' you say 'They're mine.'
You're always bragging loudly
About what you will get next
A new patio or extension
It's all on your list.
But please be quiet and listen
To what we've got to say
Your friends are tired of hearing
But you'll realise it some day
That material things don't matter
It's what you've got inside
A gift that is precious
And one you cannot hide.

Elaine Davidson

In The Shadows Of Life

It's cold and lonely in the shadows
Watching people pass me by
Needing love and affection, someone to be
there when I cry.
I've tried hard to come out of the shadows
but people always push me back
It's easy to leave me in the darkness
to remind me of the confidence I lack.
And the days when I think I see a ray of light
start to break through
There's always someone to remind me
things will go wrong, no matter what I do
So for now I'll stay in the shadows
taking comfort I can't be seen
One day I'll be happy in the light
. . . At least I can dream.

Tracy Mitchell

ORIGINAL SIN

It wasn't a happy marriage. Called into existence to keep him company,
God didn't stop to consider whether I'd actually be attracted to Adam.

I wanted stimulating discourse, but this was the man who named
such animals as: dog, cat, ant, cow . . . start to see any patterns?

I was merely Adam's 'spare rib', hardly taken seriously. I went
to the snake for Knowledge. The fruit answered my prayers;
intelligence that would make us God's equals, I thought
at least the conversation will be better.

I ate the fruit. It tasted good to be so shameful.
So I was naked, so what? I could tell Adam liked what he saw.

The relationship improved; Adam was *all* man.
But as it turned out, not man enough - to take the buck.

Ruth R Roberts

MASKS

The mask of love
    is a beautiful shade
it puts everything else into the pale.

The mask of envy
    is often met
on people who want much more, and yet!

The mask of greed
    is also there
green as grass but not so fair.

The mask of hate
    is a dreadful thing
it brings forth nought that isn't a sin.

The mask of pride
    just doesn't see
the heart that beats inside of me.

the mask of toil
    tries very hard
to bring the love-light to other's eyes.

The mask of love
    is forever there
doing its best against doom and despair.

See now the mask
    that knocks on your door
which will you take? - Can you even
                                        the score?

Beth Spinks

The Green Man

Dancing on the hillside
Catch him if you can
Glimpse him in the valley
That enigmatic man

Watch his spirit floating
On a bright moonbeam
Close your eyes and listen
See him in your dream

Hidden in the forest
Deep in groves of oak
You must stop, look and hear him
Singing songs with fairy folk

The melody will haunt you
As you journey through the trees
The wild wind blows in chorus
As it dances through the leaves

He is always there beside you
If you care to take a look
Flowing just beneath the surface
Of mountain, lake and brook

His face surrounds you everywhere
In hearth and heart and home
Carved beneath the waterfall
Etched deep within the stone

Sometimes his tears are raindrops
Gently rolling down the stone
Will he be lost forever
As he sits upon his throne

Look close and you will find him
He is waiting everywhere
Watching in the shadows
So let your heart beware

He will catch you, find you, bind you
In your heart forever more
If you stumble on life's highway
He will guide you through the door.

So if you get a glimpse of him
Catch him if you can
You will find your peace forever
In the spirit of Green Man.

David A Carter

MORNING DEW

Morning dew
falling from a star

Different hues
wherever you are

Morning mist
shrouding the view

If you persist
you will win through

Salty tears
misery arises

Tragic fears
sometimes surprises

Faith is not blind
led by true friend

Seek and you will find
faith to the end.

Mary A Shovlin

The Streets Of Swansea

I used to stroll the streets of Swansea
With the thought of seeing you
To chat awhile, to see you smile,
You'd be glad to see me too.
I still stroll the streets of Swansea,
But no longer see your face,
In the crowds all milling round me
There's no one to take your place.

When I stroll the streets of Swansea
I see the places where we'd meet,
In the gardens by the castle
We would find a shady seat
Then sit close and chat like lovers -
But that's what we'll never be,
Now you've left the streets of Swansea
And a broken-hearted me.

You wouldn't know the streets of Swansea
Now I walk them all alone.
They've been cobble-stoned and traffic-coned
And the gardens turned to stone!
Brass bands used to play there
Now tall fountains sometimes do,
One thing hasn't altered -
That's the way that I miss you!

Shirley R Thomas

WRITTEN IN THE RAIN

Sunday is here and yes it's raining,
It's October now, I only have a little garden,
It wants digging, but it would be silly in the rain,
I'll try and plan what will go in next year,
But I wonder? Will the wife agree.

Still it's raining, so watching the news,
Guess what! They have just showed us a tornado.
We don't like the rain, but tornadoes would be worse.
Evening now, still raining,
But we thank the Lord for what we've got.

Gordon E Miles

AND HIS LIFE HAD JUST BEGUN

It all seemed so easy then
With all your family and your friends,
You never seemed to worry
As no one was in a hurry.

He remembered when he was a lad
And all the great times that he had,
Going on Sunday school trips
To the seaside for a dip.

Singing in the village choir
He remembered singing so much higher,
Skimming stones across the pond
The days never seemed too long.

They used to play knock and run
In those days it was all in fun,
Scrumping apples from the trees
Hoping that no one would see.

And when the time came to go home
No one was frightened to be on their own,
Going home so happily
Just in time for your tea.

As he came back to the present
He was glad his youth had been so pleasant,
And with a smile went on his way
So glad he had another day.

K Rowe

For Rain

I'm looking through the window,
It's pouring down again.
Some people really hate it,
But I just love the rain.

Flowers tip their pretty heads,
They want to catch each drop.
Running down each grateful leaf,
Trees hope it doesn't stop.

Spots are drizzling down the glass,
Just like they're in a race.
I think I'll go outside now,
To feel it on my face.

With my eyes looking skyward,
I think I should explain.
Some people like the sunshine,
But I just love the rain.

Kaz

It

It, is always there
In darkness
Watching me fumble through thick fog.
It, sneers as I stumble
Cursing in sludge and sinking bog.
The sniggering and tittering turns to a scowl
Its eyes sharpen, fixing glare with a growl.
From out of the shadows
It, follows, it follows,
Through windy rain and misery
And dreams that I borrow.
In the thickness of the lingering fog
Its movement rumbles, rumbles,
Crashing, smashing, my stumbling blocks.
Its teeth, are clean cut sharp
Saliva drools from its gnashes
Faster, faster, fast
It, wants to devour my heart.

C Leith

Blood Bonding

We, cannot claim similitude
Of mind, looks, or attitude . . .
Clear as crystal for all to see,
We two, are simply 'chalk and cheese'
You can't subtract your life from mine,
Our DNA ties us down -
Whatever lies within the mind
Is quite mysterious and undefined.
The sacred valley of the soul,
Is the territory of God alone . . .
The kernel of our very being,
Was sealed, by Him at the beginning.
Tho polls apart, I'm still your mother . . .
Your DNA - you can't deny,
Or, that your Celtic blood flows
100% proof, just like mine!
Listen to the spoken word
It really can speak volumes -
From the mouth of babe and suckling,
Come words, worth the listening!
If, perchance, you condescend to listen . . .
Or even read these lines -
I pray, that they boost my image,
In your heart and mind!

Marion de Bruyn

Count Me In

One finger too many,
One toe too few,
These are the traits of me and you.

He's got no hair,
She has an evil stare,
Look around, who gives a care.

Little girl in special chair,
Little boy who can't behave,
Both in need of a friendly wave.

Chinese lady in foreign parts,
African man with reason to moan,
Both of them feeling all alone.

Normality is a misconception,
Belonging is a feeling from within,
But we're on the outside, looking in.

Annette Murphy

SUMMER BREEZE

Invisible fingers of a playful God
Tickle and toss nature's hair
The lightest kiss of the amorous breeze
Strokes shivers over the skin of the sea
The wind thought-of words heard soft in the night
Whisper gently in the ears of summer

James Stapleton

TELL ME

Please tell me that my life has been worthwhile
Please tell me that my morals were not crass and infantile
Tell me that I made my mark
Tell me that I mattered
Tell me that my dreams were good
Though most of them were shattered
Tell me that my actions
Were not selfish or malign
Tell me that the bad intentions
Were the masses and not mine
Please tell me that my levity
Was spoke of with affection
Not sneered at and reviled
Or thought of as deception
My allegiances are sometimes wrong
My attitudes diverse
I know that I escape my life
By writing it in verse
But this is what I am
I was made this way
Not shoved
So do not lie or fabricate
Please tell me
Was I loved?

Gavin Clements

TIMELESS

In her mind, she is with us.
All thoughts and memories there,
her body doesn't exist for her
and her movements not there, all alone in a corner
a smile, a little tear,
once a face of gladness
now an empty face of fear.
Her thoughts are of home, surviving time as
it passed,
'Don't go,' she says with sadness in her eyes.
A soul of an angel, tired because of age,
old in her body, hands of a queen,
gentle embrace, sadness and shame,
'I love you,' I cry, be back in a while,
she knows, until next time, timeless, timeless.

Lynda Hopkinson

TOMORROW

Tomorrow, if the weather's fine
We'll go off on a trip
Perhaps we'll go to Blackpool
In the sea we'll take a dip

We wake up in the morning
Through the window take a glance
The weather's not too good today
Best not take a chance

If the weather's better
We will try another day
Maybe we'll have a picnic
Or a sail around the bay

The forecast doesn't seem so good
For May, June or July
We'll wait a little longer
Then we'll have another try

August and September pass
The rain won't go away
Looks like we won't get the chance
To have a holiday

Oh well! Perhaps tomorrow
We might just see the sun
But you've guessed! Just like tomorrow
English summer never comes!

Joan M Jones

Dyslexia

So many thoughts
within my soul,
So many feelings
in dark turmoil.

So many words
within my head,
So many lines
now left unsaid.

So many things
I'd like to say,
So many ideas
in such disarray.

So many stanzas
yet to write,
So many prose
just take flight.

So many poems
I'd love to share,
But simple there is
nothing there!

Andy Whitfield

The Inevitable

As once again there's talk of war,
When will all fighting cease?
The pacifists shout out anew
'Why can't we live in peace?'

Young men and women, daughters, sons,
With all their life to live,
As they, their country's name defend,
Their lives, their all, they give.

Satanical tyrants lust for power,
Oppressive, harsh despots,
Their sole reliance for their ends
Are bombs and rifle shots.

They do not care 'pon whom they tread
To reach their final goal,
Or who they hurt or maim or kill
As long as they control.

Yet this was prophesied of old
Two thousand years ago,
Before the end of time does come,
These wars we all must know.

Colin Ross

In My Mind

All around, inside my head
the music starts to play
faint and fragile, seems to be
a soundtrack to the day

I see couples laugh and dance
caught in rhythm's hold
romance simmers in the air
the melody grows bold

In my room, with open eyes
the darkness lingers on
four blank walls, no hope in sight
sorrow's endless song

But in my mind, with eyes shut tight
I share the joy and peace
the place my thoughts are taking me
makes all memories cease

I long to join them, take myself
follow my searching soul
leave my pain in this small room
give my mind control

I feel the physical resist
but hope creates the chance
miracles can happen, slip through
join the unseen dance

On my bed, an empty shell
lays in darkness vast
while all of me that wants to live
stays within the past

So, in the room that I escaped
there remains naught but dreams
echoes of a time of warmth
when all was as it seems

Debra Kessing

OUR LOVED ONES ARE NEAR

When our loved ones pass over
and it's time for them to depart.
We are left feeling empty and lonely,
with a great pain in our heart.
They haven't gone far,
they are there, beside you.
They'll give us some proof,
also fond memories too.
Whether a colour, a familiar smell,
or a favourite song that you hear.
It's their way of saying,
'I'm not gone. I'm still here.'
It may be a warmth,
or a tickle on the face.
They've come in so close,
and with love you they embrace.
It may be their favourite chair
or a door you hear creek.
Please don't run and hide,
stay strong, don't be weak.
They want you there,
and for you to stay strong.
It's their way of showing,
to you they still belong.
It's just our loved ones in the spirit world,
showing us they are still there.
They are still around us and it's
their way of showing they still care.
When it's our time to depart,
and cross over too.
All our loved ones will be waiting,
arms stretched out, with love just for you.

When it's our time to pass over,
and our bodies switch off the light.
We will go to the spirit world,
where we all will shine bright . . .

Diane Ennis-Chopping & Leau Chie

Sorry

I look so hard but I cannot find,
A single way to turn back time,
But I have a lot upon my mind,
And this is why I wrote this rhyme,
I wish I didn't do some things I've done,
I should never have hurt you I know,
But if I don't tell you this, then evil has won,
And I will feel very low,
I never meant to hurt you bad,
I love you really much,
I didn't mean to make you mad,
And break everything I touch,
I didn't mean to curse and swear,
Or tell lies just to hurt you,
I know I told you I didn't care,
When it is clear I really do,
I didn't mean to let you down,
And completely break your trust,
I don't like it how I made you frown,
Even though I whined and fussed,
I made you feel guilty and blamed you,
When I knew it wasn't your fault,
I sometimes told you I hated you,
To give your heart an awful jolt,
But now you're gone it's too late to tell you,
I miss your voice and your touch,
My pain and regrets are so true,
I'm sorry and love you so much!

Lisa Booth

THE SONG OF THE CUCKOO

Joy to the world
In the middle of May,
The cuckoo bird sits
On a hawthorn spray;
The weathervane veers,
And the pendulum rocks,
Silver threepenny bits,
In my old money box
Santa's down the chimney,
The pudding's on fire.
That old overhead projector,
He never seems to tire.
When we herald our maker,
With spirits aglow.
We'll forget that we cried,
When the bird had to go.

Jennifer Hawthorne

Election Time

Smiling nicely, shaking hands
Walking the pavements day by day
Trying to please by listening and helping
Who will give support; who'll say?

Headlines to choose for a newsletter
Looking well, dressing up for photos
Thanking deliverers, hope they'll stay fit
Look after those feet, they'll need it.

Nominations must be completed
Ten names collected; just right
Only those sign who are eligible
Make no mistake, or a chore to repeat.

Soon there'll be knocking on doors,
Wondering who's watching left or right.
Who's at home? All quiet - put a card through.
Mind the noisy dog; will he bite?

Plenty of people, their views to seek
Many are kind and happy supporters,
Others say no; they prefer another colour.
Some express no interest; they won't vote.

Waiting ends when Election Day comes
Charming sitting room, so cosy and quiet;
Changed to 'Committee Room' unfamiliar and busy
People in and out all day and night.

Finally, candidates arrive for the count
Officers and clerks are on duty opening boxes,
All must wait patiently to hear the results,
What a long night, after a day far too long.

Now the Chief Executive announces winning names.
Every detail written and correct for the media;
Congratulations for the victors and kisses from friends
Home to bed at 3am and rest those weary feet.

Sheila Rowland

A World On The Edge

A world is lost, a star left with no hope.
Ashes to ashes,
Oblivion to oblivion . . .
Man has become so destructive, in his will to dominate.
He cares not for the future,
Only for his immediate pleasures and dominion over others.
Wars will ensue,
Security counsels will gather,
In order to protect our petroleum lives.
But sooner than that, our fate is decided:
Closed doors behind cloaks of secrecy,
Our fates in the wrong hands,
Our demise assured.
Hope is but a delusion of the truth:
The truth we have no control in our lives.
A date is set,
But the fear is stolen from us.
Like fattened pigs to the slaughter,
We serve to feed those 'higher' than us:
A caste society of self-interested rulers
And consumerist producers.
But who survives?
Not us.
For we cannot afford our salvation:
Our tax saves our destroyers the world over,
So they can fight for a charred wasteland,
Once called Eden,
Once called Earth . . .
Now with no name,
For it has no life.
Like Mars, we too shall become Gods of War
And ravage our fertile planet.
I will not cry for us.
My pain shall not be heard,
For others are disinterested in it.

So I forget without regret,
And cherish these days . . .
For even the might of an entire population
Cannot overcome our rulers,
Cannot overcome our greed . . .
Contempt for contempt,
The cycle repeats.
Then we are destroyers . . .
Accept our fate,
For it is out of our hands.
Buy into the delusions:
They are the only hope you have.

Alan Garfoot

NEW BORN

Nothing can match
That first flutter
The first twinkling of an eye
When two people have
Become one
The ultimate bonding
Of a love so pure
X and Y are joined
But five months ago
Then suddenly the
First kick for space
One body becomes two
Living off the other
Unable to survive without
The other
The first sounds of the
Beating heart
Blares out like a
Fanfare
Flesh distorts so another
May grow
Is it a leg, an arm
A shoulder?
Who knows, who cares?
As long as it keeps
Moving
A steady rhythmic thump
Means too much to drink
Hush now, eight months
That can hear
Stretching, kicking, trying
To make more space
Trying as best it can
To find comfort

It's quite still now
Too big for exercises
A sudden tightening
Means at last it can
Make its exit
Pushing, panting,
Sweating
Inch by inch
A bit of hair, the top of the head
A face!
Then suddenly
Finally
It's there, a family
Greasy and pink
But cherished at once
Sucking for life
Gasping for breath
Crying for the world.

Lorna Jones

EPOCH

Once there was one
Now there is none

Collection of individuals
Epoch of ideals

Now a vacuous space
An empty faceless mass

Killing for smack
They are never going on the rack

Carefree antics of violent addicts
Crazed special cases running amok

Elderly prisons for dying
Bars on windows scenic views

Liberal culture working wonders
Tell that to the dead and scared

Community is a cultural myth
It never occurred and never will

As a nation we are individuals
As an individual we think of ourselves

Ian Todd

Quack

Quack the name given to a doctor
Quack the voice of the duck and drake
Both have gifts of healing
The human kind will prescribe medicine and pills
Therapy to cure your ills
The best cure is the quack on the pond
Water runs off his back
He paddles the water with his webbed feet
Feed him with your stale bread -
That really is a treat.

Christine M Wicks

MINDLESS

They need to scratch that itch with somebody

Tongue is in motion
Mindless chatter
Thrust the knife into your neighbour's back

Not with metal, with cruel words.
See the blood and smile.

Passes time
No harm done.
A sort of sport.
A blood sport.

But, do you smile, when they knife you?

No.
You rage injustice.
You seek revenge.
Bigot.

Dig my grave, and you dig your own
Twice as fast.

Mind you don't fall in.

Lindsey Susan Powell

No Matter You

And what to say on the sea? On the depths to come?
The water's getting high, but always reflects the sun.
Some bricks are missing, someone's waiting outside.
Somewhere out there, a star just died.
People trying to work away, with other things on their mind.
Bosses wanna put feet down, can't find no crime.
People handing out leaflets with nothing on.
Spare change from the bottom of the fountain is gone.
Gaps in the skyline, in front of me . . . Dad I'm so glad you stopped going to sea.
And so hard it is not to walk to the beat you're listening to,
Pain and again and again we're walking through.
And dancin' on pennies, same shape as the world we're on . . .
What's the world coming to? What's it coming from?
People handing out leaflets in all the wrong places.
And always missing the last one that's covering their faces.
They may say, 'You'll never reach the top my dear . . .'
Just drop ya cup, interrupt and say, 'Can't hear ya from up here!'
See it's the way you see it (or if you see at all).
No matter you big or small, you still fall.
But don't bow that head to my point of view, and don't tilt that hat . . .
We'll fall to the same ground . . . Dad taught me that.
So some are working away, some are working bricks,
One is singing, some are playing tricks.
And one day we shall all look on the distance, on the horizon . . .
They'll say, 'What a nice sunset.' We'll say, 'What a nice sun rising.'
Y'know some say two hearts live better from being away for time . . .
'Absence makes the heart grow fonder?' Well, absence broke mine.
Gaps in the skyline in front of me . . . Dad I'm so glad you stopped going to sea.

Dave Skelton

Log Floating

Log floating
on the ebb tide,
its hundredweights
heaved out from the root,
routed to the sea.

See now
on the river's weariness
dreadnought buoyancy,
a geometry in its slowness,
it went out beyond reach.

Earth sprawls
in this slab, the pith arms
dead now to the leaves,
leave something in the
cayman silence of its floating.

Uncompromising,
the river hold it to itself,
rocked on the consummate
gravity of water.

Earth turns so
its season on returning,
is my returning, sometime,
as surely, I know.

Richard Ball